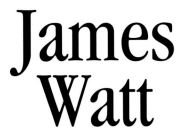

James Watt

Master of the Steam Engine

Anna Sproule

BLACKBIRCH PRESS, INC.

WOODBRIDGE, CONNECTICUT

Published by Blackbirch Press, Inc.
260 Amity Road
Woodbridge, CT 06525
Web site: http://www.blackbirch.com
e-mail: staff@blackbirch.com

© 2001 Blackbirch Press, Inc.
First U.S. Edition

First published in Great Britain as *Scientists Who Have Changed the World* by Exley Publications Ltd., Chalk Hill, Watford, 1992.
© Exley Publications, Ltd., 1992
© Anna Sproule, 1992

10 9 8 7 6 5 4 3 2 1

Photo Credits:
Bridgeman Art Library: 18, 36 (Oldham Art Library), 37, 52 (top Science Museum), 54 (top Gavin Graham Gallery), 55; e.t. archive: 12-3, 44 (Science Museum), 50; Mary Evans Picture Library: 9, 13, 27, 43; Guildhall Library: 11; Hulton Picture Company: 5, 10, 15, 19, 20 (both), 22, 33, 48 (below), 52 (below); Image Bank: 30 below (P. Bartholomew/Liais), 58 (Jake Rajs), 59 (P&G Bowater); Mansell Collection: 40, 48 (top); National Portrait Gallery, London: Cover; Portfolio Pictures: 6, 16, 39, 41 (National Portrait Gallery), 54 (below); Ann Ronan Picture Library: 4 (both), 7 (both), 19, 21, 23, 25, 28-9, 51 (below); Tate Gallery Publications: 30.

Printed in China

Library of Congress Cataloging-in-Publication Data

Sproule, Anna.
    James Watt: master of the steam engine / Anna Sproule.
        p. cm. — (Giants of science)
Includes bibliographical references and index.
Summary: A biography of the eighteenth-century Scottish inventor and engineer whose improved designs of the steam engine made its wide use possible.
    ISBN 1-56711-338-9 (alk. paper)
    1. Watt, James 1736-1819—Juvenile literature. 2. Mechanical engineers—Great Britain—Biography—Juvenile literature. [1. Watt, James, 1736-1819. 2. Inventors.] I. Title. II. Series.

TJ140.W38 S67 2001   2001035462
621'.092—dc21   CIP
                                                                          AC

Contents

Two paintings from the late 1700s show iron ore mines. The tall chimneys in the painting stand over engine houses that were built to operate Watt's pumps. His invention made it possible for mines to be dug in areas that were once believed to be too wet.

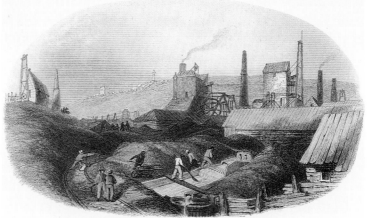

The Miners' Enemy

The miners of the Cornwall mining region in England hated water. So did anyone else in the eighteenth century that worked beneath the ground, hacking coal or iron ore out of the earth. Underground water was the enemy of miners. It oozed from tunnel walls and dripped like rain from the tunnel roofs. Miners knelt in it, even lay in it to do their backbreaking work. If the water became too deep, work stopped completely.

Until the 1700s, children too small to handle a pick yet big enough to carry a bucket had removed underground floodwater from mines. As mines sank deeper, however, they became wetter. By the mid-1700s, machines had taken over the work of removing water from the mines.

Most British mines had steam-powered pumps set at the edge of the pit shafts. The pumps' mechanical arms rocked from morning till night, pumping water up from tunnels below. Machine pumps modernized the mining industry, but they were unreliable, slow, and dangerous. They were also expensive to run. Heating water until it boiled produced the steam that worked the pump. To do this, large amounts of coal were needed for fuel.

In 1776, the owners of Wheal Bay mine in Cornwall heard of a new pumping engine that worked faster and used less coal. The new pump was manufactured by Boulton & Watt of Birmingham. Wheal Bay's owners ordered one and, when its parts arrived, so did the man who would supervise the setup—James Watt, the inventor of the new machine.

This engraving of James Watt was made in the 1700s when he had become a leading figure in science and industry.

The beam engine installed at the Wheal Bay mine was the first in a long line of Watt engines. The rotating beam engine shown here was built in 1788 for use as a pump.

. . . .

"The velocity, violence, magnitude and horrible noise of the engine gives universal satisfaction to all beholders."

James Watt, describing reactions to his pumping engine.

. . . .

Fast, Cheap, Powerful

The slim, soft-spoken Watt did not impress the rugged miners of Cornwall, and few believed his claims for his new pumping engine. In fact, the Boulton & Watt machine looked like the pump already in use. But Wheal Bay would soon show other Cornish miners the truth. In September, 1777, the moment of truth arrived.

After a few demonstrations, the miners could see that Watt's pump worked faster and used much less coal. How much less, the watchers gathered around the engine-house didn't quite know. But it was something like a third of what they had used, perhaps even a quarter. That meant big savings for the mine owner, and no one who saw it in action could deny its power.

Deafening Roar

As the roaring machine continued emptying the flooded tunnel below, the Cornish miners smiled and shouted congratulations to their Scottish expert. Bowing and smiling, James Watt shouted something back about the reason the pump worked so well. But the racket of his machine drowned out his words.

Chances were, few men of Watt's day would have understood the beauty of the machine anyway. They thought the young Scot's achievement was just a matter of noise, size, and cost cutting. But the truth, he knew, was different. He had cut their costs while building the most powerful steam engine the world had ever known. Watt also knew that he had changed the whole method of harnessing steam's enormous power.

Watt did not know, however, that he had created something that would change the world.

The Baby Survived

James Watt was born on January 19, 1736, in Scotland, in the small port of Greenock near the mouth of the River Clyde. His father had originally trained as a carpenter and could build anything from furniture to ships.

Mr. Watt's business sense and skills brought in good money for his family. Although not rich, he and his wife Agnes were comfortably off. They needed that comfort because their home life was filled with tragedy—several of their children had died in infancy.

When James was born, his mother was determined to protect her baby from the many illnesses that threatened children in those days. She succeeded with James, though he grew up as a thin, sickly boy. Throughout his childhood, he suffered from migraine headaches and toothaches, which

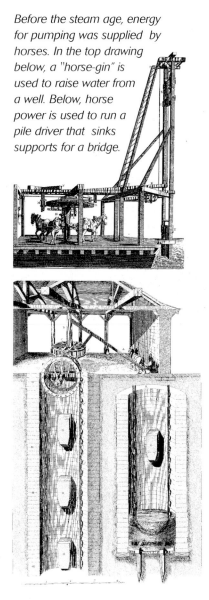

Before the steam age, energy for pumping was supplied by horses. In the top drawing below, a "horse-gin" is used to raise water from a well. Below, horse power is used to run a pile driver that sinks supports for a bridge.

affected his moods. Some days he'd be talkative, friendly, and interested in everything around him. Other days he'd be lost in a haze of pain.

Playground Bullies

James was intelligent, but his health problems kept him from attending school. Instead, his parents, both well educated, taught him at home. Agnes taught her son to read. His busy father made time to give him lessons in writing and arithmetic. He also gave James a small carpentry set. Young James used the tools to take all his toys apart and then put them back together.

When James was eleven, his happy, sheltered situation came to an end. He had to attend public school. Nothing in his life had prepared him for the noise, the teasing, and the rough-and-tumble play of the schoolyard.

The small boy didn't understand the jokes, and didn't know how to join in the games. For protection, he kept to himself, but this made him a target for playground bullies. He escaped them when he changed schools at thirteen. But the emotional marks those two years left on him—shyness, self-doubt, and uncertainty—would not disappear until he was a respected and wealthy older man.

His Gifts Surface

By age thirteen, the worst of James's miseries were behind him. In the safer, calmer surroundings of Greenock Grammar School, James let his gifts surface. Quickly, he blossomed into an outstanding mathematics student. Out of school, he began to learn the family trade as a builder.

James had inherited his father's skill as a craftsman. Many people thought James could make anything—out of almost any material. The best work he did was precise, delicate metalwork.

Mr. Watt was a ship-owner and merchant as well as a builder. He also bought and sold navigation aids such as quadrants, compasses, and telescopes. James learned how to use them and how to repair them. By his mid-teens his heart was set on becoming a maker of scientific instruments. He wasn't interested in being a carpenter or a shipwright like his father.

Making scientific instruments was skilled work that demanded training. Unfortunately, there was no one in Greenock to train him. Glasgow, his mother's home, offered more possibilities. So, in 1754, James left Greenock to see what the city had to offer.

Going to Glasgow turned out to be a good choice at first. Agnes Watt's maiden name had been Muirhead, a well-known name in Glasgow. George Muirhead taught at the university, and it is through

This famous painting by Marcus Stone shows the young James Watt observing condensed steam pouring out of a boiling kettle.

this university connection that Watt made many important and longlasting contacts.

One connection was Robert Dick, a scientist who liked James right away and gave him a temporary job setting up scientific instruments in a laboratory. When it came to getting trained in instrument building, however, James found that, like Greenock, no one in the city could do it.

Off to London

Dick, noticing James's skill and intelligence, told his young friend that he was wasting his time in Glasgow. London was the place to be. Back in Greenock, Watt's father—who had fallen on hard times—agreed to the plan even though he could not help his son with expenses. Robert Dick wrote to a London instrument maker he knew, urging him to take James on as his trainee.

James packed his possessions and put them on a London-bound ship. Then he bought a horse and set out on the long road south to London. He arrived in mid-June 1755. Dick's friend, James Short, was decent, helpful, and a master of his craft. But he could not take Watt into his business. Nor could anyone else.

James trudged around the city, visiting one training shop after another. Every time, it was the same story. He had come up against the Worshipful Company of Clock makers.

A Vicious Cycle

The Worshipful Company made the rules governing London's instrument-making trade. One rule stated that qualified instrument-makers could only take two types of people into their business. The first type was other qualified instrument-makers. The second type was apprentices to serve a seven-year training period.

This drawing shows an instrument-maker at work. Every part of a clock, watch, or other measuring device had to be made by hand. It was work that demanded great accuracy and concentration.

Watt was not qualified. And unless a London business took him on, he would never qualify. Yet, the only way to qualify was by serving an apprenticeship. Watt, almost twenty, was too old to become an apprentice.

The young Watt felt trapped by this system of regulations. He'd come all this way for nothing. Yet there was nothing for him back home, either. Meanwhile, his money was running out.

Just when things were looking their worst, James Short came up with another contact. His name was John Morgan, his trade was brasswork, and he had a business in the very heart of London. Morgan had a defiant attitude toward the Worshipful Company's rules. Young Watt, he said, was welcome to join his business. But there was a catch. The trainee was to work for his master free of charge for a year. In addition, he was to pay Morgan a "training fee."

"We work to nine o'clock every night, except Saturdays."

James Watt, writing to his father from London, 1756.

This sketch of the Cornhill area of London shows the place where John Morgan finally gave James a chance to learn the instrument maker's trade.

Free labor and a training fee was not ideal, but Watt jumped at the chance. Right away, Morgan spotted Watt's talent. By August, the unofficial trainee had outperformed Morgan's official apprentice, who had been there two years. By the following spring, Watt had begun to repair surveying instruments on his own.

Overworked, Undernourished

Watt, however, paid a price for his success. Trying to cram several years of training into one, the young man worked ten-hour days, working until late evening most days including Saturday. Exhausted, he'd get up very early to fit in some

extra work that brought in a tiny amount of cash. Together with the tiny allowance his father sent, it was barely enough to live on.

Overworked and undernourished, Watt needed exercise and fresh air. Both would have done him good. But at that time, Britain was at war with France. The British Navy wanted men—and they didn't wait for people to volunteer! To make up shortages, press gangs scoured the streets and kidnapped any reasonably fit man they could find. Often, these "volunteers" were never seen again. Watt, thin as he was, would have been fair game. So, month after month, he stayed out of sight in Morgan's cold workshops.

Watt completed his training year in triumph. But in the summer of 1756, his health broke down completely. Rheumatism, migraines, and crushing fatigue set in. All were made worse by poor working conditions and shabby living arrangements. He knew that he had to get home to recover his health. Packing his clothes, tools, and a precious book on instrument-making in his saddlebags, twenty-year-old Watt slowly made his way back to Scotland and to Greenock.

Once back, Watt recovered both his health and spirits. Later that year, he returned to Glasgow to find that Robert Dick had a splendid project waiting for him. A valuable collection of astronomical instruments had recently arrived from Jamaica—but the weeks at sea in salt-filled air had harmed the delicate metalwork. Watt was given the job of returning the instruments to working condition, an ideal task for the young craftsman.

Watt was paid five pounds for his work, a large sum at the time. But his real reward lay in the work itself, and in the new friends he made while he was doing it. The Jamaica collection fascinated Glasgow's scientists, who often came to watch the work. Naturally, they also got to know the technician in charge, and they found he was as knowledgeable as any university man.

Out of His Shell

One of Watt's new acquaintances was a student of mathematics and mechanics, John Robison. Another was Joseph Black, a distinguished scientist who'd just been appointed professor of chemistry. Despite his reputation, Black was young, only ten years older than Robison. The professor and the pupil, who first met in Watt's workshop, both got along well with Watt, who fell between them in age. Black liked the gifted technician's "simplicity" and

. . . .

"He [James Watt] was as remarkable for the goodness of his heart, and the candor and simplicity of his mind, as for the acuteness of his genius and understanding."

Professor Black

. . . .

. . . .

"I had the vanity to think myself a pretty good proficient in my favorite study, and was rather mortified at finding Mr. Watt so much my superior. But his own high relish for those things made him pleased with the chat of any person who had the same tastes as himself . . . I lounged much about him, and, I doubt not, was frequently teasing him. Thus our acquaintance began."

John Robison, describing how he first met James Watt

. . . .

14

good nature. Robison—a cheerful character— became Watt's friend on the spot. The conversation, the admiration and, above all, the shared delight in science brought Watt out of his shell and allowed him to form these lifetime friendships.

The following year, Watt decided to set up shop as an instrument-maker in the city he now called home. In one way, however, Glasgow was just like London. The Glasgow craftsmen also had their city tightly controlled. Watt was not a Glasgow man, nor had he served his apprenticeship in Glasgow. The message he received from the other Glasgow instrument-makers was clear: keep out!

Luckily, his university friends came to his aid, just as they had done before he went to London. This time, however, they changed the course of his life. The Glasgow craftsmen had no power over people employed by the university itself. The professors arranged for Watt to set up shop on the university grounds. Then they made it official by giving him the title "Mathematical Instrument Maker to the University."

An Outsider No Longer

Thus Watt, trained in the most uncertain and unofficial ways, was an outsider no longer. From then on, he played a growing role in the scientific achievement that arose in Britain and the western world. The only trouble was that his new job did not earn him enough to live on. Watt studied his market and decided to enlarge his business by making musical instruments as well as scientific ones. Watt was not a musician. His mathematical abilities and crafting skills, however, served him well. Soon, an amazing range of instruments began to come out of his workshops: harps, flutes, bagpipes, and even organs—not the standard type of organ, either, but an improved model.

This engraving shows Dr. Joseph Black, professor of chemistry at Glasgow University. Black and Watt were lifelong friends.

As a child, Watt had taken his toys apart and re-fashioned them to make new ones. Now, as an adult, the urge to tinker, to improve, to explore was as strong as ever. The stops on a Watt organ, for example, functioned more efficiently than those of the traditional type. A Watt organ made better use of the air that was pumped through it.

A Tricky Job

Two years later, when Watt was still in his early twenties, a prosperous and friendly architect gave him a loan to open another shop in the city itself. This time, the other Glasgow instrument-makers didn't object. By 1763, Watt's business had grown big enough for him to take on apprentices of his own. But he still kept his university shop open. It was to this shop that Professor John Anderson came in the winter of 1763 with a repair job that had baffled the finest engineers and instrument makers in London. Anderson learned that Watt was at least their equal, if not better.

By this time, Watt's first patron, Dr. Dick, had died. Anderson was his successor, and he was just as impressed by Watt as Dick had been. He explained that the job he wanted done was especially tricky. Watt, always hungry for problems to solve, accepted the challenge eagerly. Anderson handed this latest challenge over—a model of a Newcomen pump.

Watt knew of the pump. So did anyone in the eighteenth century who was interested in machines. Without it, the mining industry would never have been transformed from backbreaking manual labor to the booming industry it had become. Watt had another reason for taking on the challenge. He was interested in the unusual way the pump was powered. Since he'd first played with his parents' teapot, steam had fascinated him.

Opposite: *This painting shows the original building of Glasgow University where James Watt worked as the "Mathematical Instrument Maker to the University."*

17

Muscles, Wind, and Water

Throughout history, farmers, craftspeople, and soldiers had invented and improved tools to help them do their jobs. But, until less than a hundred years earlier, they had known only three main ways to power those tools.

The oldest and simplest method was muscle power—the movements of a farmer cutting corn or a blacksmith hammering a horseshoe. The horse that wore the shoes provided another source of muscle power, as did donkeys and oxen. Animals were stronger than humans, and animal power was used to work the fields, grind corn, pull carts, or draw water from wells.

Horses, however, were expensive animals. All animals used for power needed housing, doctoring, and feeding—especially feeding. And growing the grain to feed the animals required land—a resource not always available. Two other sources of power were much simpler and less time-consuming to care for, once the equipment had been set up. Those were wind and water.

Opposite top: *Before the 1700s, farming required a large workforce. Sometimes, an entire community worked together during harvest time.*

Bottom: *Before steam power, windmills were used to raise water and drive machinery. Wind, however, was often unpredictable, and windmills were not dependable.*

Below: *A water mill was a common sight in Watt's day. Like windmills, however, these depended on forces of nature. Droughts and floods could put a mill wheel out of action.*

19

Wind, captured in the sails of a windmill, was as good as a horse for turning millstones or pumping up water from underground. Water, channeled over water wheels placed across a stream, could turn millstones and other equipment in just the same way. Wind and water, brought together in the sailing ship, provided one of the most efficient transport methods then known.

Natural Power

Muscle power, wind power, or water power could all be efficient if properly harnessed. These methods still work in many areas of the world. Even today—in countries with thin, fragile soils—a traditional animal plow will not damage the land as much as a western-style tractor. In countries with fast-flowing rivers, hydroelectric plants generate electricity for millions of homes.

Yet, all these sources of power have one weakness: They are ultimately controlled by nature, not by their users. The wind can weaken. A river can dry up in summer or freeze in winter. A human being worked too hard will collapse from exhaustion. And, in places where there are no fields for grazing, animals cannot be used.

For centuries, those who used powered equipment accepted these problems as unavoidable. There was nothing they could do except make the

Muscle power drove the coal industry in the eighteenth century. Because mine tunnels were so narrow, children were often given the job of hauling coal from underground.

Opposite: *This sketch shows Savery's "Miner's Friend," the first steam pump used in coal mines.*

best of it. Then, at the end of the 1600s, a new source of power was unleashed. This new power source would one day eliminate the dependence on nature. In Britain, Thomas Savery announced that he had developed a new power source and that he had solved the problem of the flooded mines.

The World's First Pump

Savery's solution was a pump that worked independently of wind, weather, and the aching muscles of tired people or animals. It would go on working as hard and as long as its operators wished. Savery called it an "engine to raise water by fire."

Actually, the engine was not powered by fire, but by water heated to its boiling point over a fire. That is, water that had been turned into steam. Savery's "Miner's Friend," which he patented in 1698, was the world's first practical steam engine.

Patented though it was, the pump was not the first steam-powered machine. As far back as the first century AD, Hero of Alexandria, a Greek scientist had described the workings of a toy steam turbine. That machine twirled round and round as steam inside it escaped. Hero's toy worked because of the way water changes when it is boiled. It turns to vapor and expands to about 1,700 times its liquid size.

Later, investigators found another method of using steam to drive machinery. This method relied not just on the effects of heating water, but also on what happens when vaporized water is suddenly cooled again—a sudden vacuum forms that can be instantly filled by any liquid or gas that has access to it.

Using this second method, Savery designed a machine to suck up a liquid—water—from a flooded mine. It was a simple idea. The design was too simple, however, and the machine only worked at

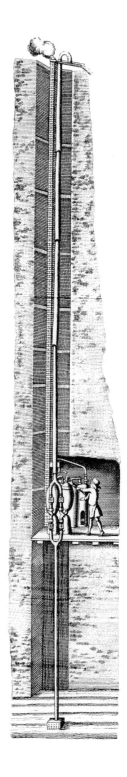

Opposite: *This sketch shows the design of Newcomen's engine with its domed boiler sitting beneath the cylinder. When the cylinder filled with steam, a piston raised a rod that pushed the beam up. That movement formed a vacuum in the cylinder, causing the piston to fall, and the cycle to begin again.*

Below: *The Newcomen engine in the photo, installed in a Scottish factory in 1730, was still working in 1908 when the photo was taken. The engine was the first to be widely used for pumping water from mine pits as well as for lifting miners and material.*

shallow depths. It was not long before a second improved pump came on the scene. Its inventor was a blacksmith named Thomas Newcomen.

The Newcomen Pump

The "atmospheric engine" built by Newcomen in 1712 was more complicated than Savery's machine. With a domed boiler, brick engine housing, and a seesawing beam connected to heavy pump rods, it was also much bigger. Its heart was an iron cylinder over the boiler. When the water boiled, the cylinder filled with the steam it made.

Although the cylinder was open at the top, it had a moving "lid" inside. This was a piston, a circular plate packed with leather that fit the cylinder exactly, yet was still free to slide up and down. It was attached to a vertical rod—the piston rod—and this was fastened to one end of the pump's handle with the rocking-beam balanced overhead.

When the cylinder below the piston filled with steam, the weight of the pump rods pulled the other end of the beam down. At the cylinder end, the beam rose up and, at the same time, the piston was dragged up to rest just inside the cylinder's rim. Pulling the "pump-handle" down meant pushing the piston down to the bottom of the cylinder again. This was where the vacuum method came in.

Condensed Steam

The vacuum produced by the cooling, condensing steam in Newcomen's pump did not directly move anything up or down. Instead, the opposite took place. The vacuum made it possible for the moving to be done by air.

Newcomen sprayed the inside walls of a cylinder with cold water to cool the steam in the cylinder. The steam condensed, creating a vacuum. With literally nothing in the cylinder, the air exerted pressure on the piston, driving it down into the cylinder. As the piston moved down, it dragged the rocking-beam down with it.

This process moved the pump-handle into the "down" position. Then, when steam entered the cylinder again to destroy the vacuum, it moved up again. And down. Then up and down again, as long as the machinery and the fuel supply held out. The

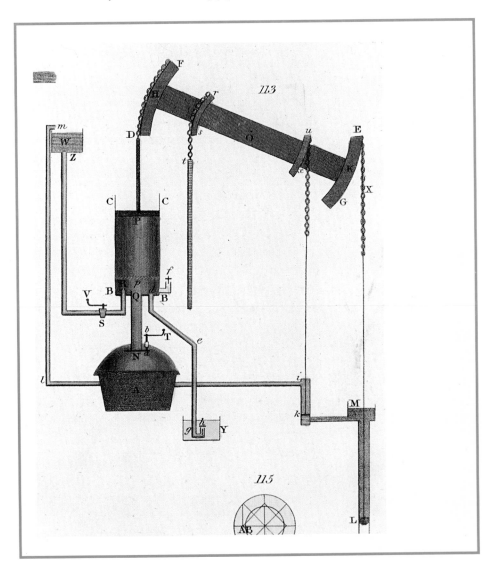

problem was that the rapid heating and cooling caused wear in the metal of the cylinder. A small crack could stop the machine; a larger one could mean disaster.

Savery had pointed the way. But it was Thomas Newcomen who had actually given the world its first alternative source of power. In doing so, he had started a process that would transform the manner in which work was done.

The Machine Stopped

Although Watt knew all about the Newcomen pump, he'd never actually seen one. Delighted with the opportunity, he took the model from Anderson and set it up on his workbench. He examined its beam and pump rod, its tiny boiler, and its neatly tooled cylinder with its piston and valves. Then he set to work. As winter settled in, the job neared completion. Soon, the little pump was repaired and ready for testing.

Robison was there to watch the tests take place. The boiler was filled, the fire below it was lit, and the steam began to build up. With the two men watching intently, the little piston began to move up and down, working the beam fixed to the strut above. Four strokes . . . five strokes . . . six . . . Watt and Robison smiled with satisfaction as the machine puttered on. But then the puttering stopped.

Watt was puzzled. The model had been working. What had gone wrong? He tried one solution after another—stoking up the fire, raising the level of the water tank perched high above the apparatus. But nothing made a difference. The model repaired by Watt worked, but only for a few strokes.

As Watt's experiments on the model continued, he slowly realized what had happened. It was not his work. The problem lay in the pump's design. The full-scale Newcomen engine was notorious for the huge amounts of fuel it consumed. The strange way the model behaved was related to this very problem. Its miniature boiler could not produce enough steam to work the pump.

The model was now as close to working as it ever could be. But to a problem-lover like Watt, the puzzles that arose from it couldn't be set aside so easily. Why, he wondered, did the machine need so much fuel and use so much steam?

The only way to find out was to try things for himself, Watt concluded. So he began to piece together the laws that governed steam and the way it behaved. And, as he did so, he realized just what was wrong with Newcomen's original design.

Too Much Heat

Both the miniature model and the full-size fuel-greedy engine used too much heat. That was the way it was designed. With each stroke of the

In this drawing, James Watt studies the Newcomen engine in his Glasgow laboratory. Watt's improvement to the engine made it more reliable while it used less fuel.

engine, the steam-filled cylinder had to be cooled to the point where the steam condensed. Then, right away, the cylinder had to be heated up again by steam rushing into it from below. That steam had to be heated to the point where it did not condense.

No wonder the model pump had not worked, Watt realized. Not only was it hard on the metal, it simply could not handle the heating and re-heating! And no wonder the full-sized engine used such huge amounts of fuel. Despite its great value, the world's first effective steam engine was flawed by an error in its design.

Watt had at last found a challenge worthy of his talents. Everything depended on the way the vacuum was created, he reasoned. That vacuum resulted from condensing steam that had filled the cylinder. To produce it, that steam had to be suddenly cooled—by the water sprayed from the machine's injection jet. The cylinder, of course, was cooled too.

Watt wondered whether there was any way of producing a vacuum without cooling the cylinder. He turned the problem over in his mind for months: no cooling, no vacuum. No vacuum, no pump.

Walk on Glasgow Green

The final solution came suddenly to Watt, between one breath and the next while he was taking a Sunday afternoon walk. On a beautiful day in May 1765, Watt decided to take a stroll. A gentle wind blew, shaking the bushes around Glasgow Green. The green was really a big meadow on the riverbank, a grazing area for sheep. The city's washerwomen came here to bleach their sheets in the sun. Many other Scots came here to walk by the river and enjoy the fresh air. Dressed in his Sunday best, and driven from his workbench by

"One Sunday afternoon I had gone to take a walk in the Green of Glasgow, and when about half way between the Herd's House and Arn's Well, my thoughts having been naturally turned to the experiments I had been engaged in for saving heat in the cylinder, at that part of the road the idea occurred to me, that, as steam was an elastic vapor, it would expand, and rush into a previously exhausted space; and that, if I were to produce a vacuum in a separate vessel, and open a communication between the steam in the cylinder and the exhausted vessel, such would be the consequence."

James Watt

the strict Scottish rules against working on Sunday, Watt had come to take in the air.

He was now married, but on this day, his wife Margaret had stayed home. Wandering along on his own, deep in thought, he passed the building that the washerwomen used, then the house where the shepherd lived. Suddenly it came to him—the solution to the whole problem.

This painting shows Glasgow in the 1700s. By that time, Glasgow had become Scotland's second largest city, due to its location as a key port for Atlantic shipping trade.

The Separate Container

Steam had no shape. Because of this, it would rush into any empty container that enclosed a vacuum. Suppose such a container, equipped with an injection jet, was attached to the engine's cylinder? The steam would rush into that, and be cooled there. In other words, Watt saw, the all-important cooling and condensing process would take place in a separate part of the engine altogether.

As the steam condensed in the separate chamber, more steam would come rushing in, to be condensed in its turn. This would be followed by more steam, until all the steam in the cylinder had been sucked into the condensing chamber. And all that would then be left in the still-hot cylinder would be a vacuum, ready for air pressure to play its role.

That was the answer he had been searching for. A separate container he called the condenser was the key to the puzzle that had eluded him. A condenser would produce the vacuum needed for the pumping action and keep the cylinder hot at the same time. Now, only one question remained. How could he get rid of the water once it was condensed?

Early Monday morning, Watt was at his work-bench, working with a soldering iron. There was no time for careful, painstaking craft. On this day, improvisation ruled.

When he needed something small and round to stop one end of a pipe, Watt used his wife's sewing thimble. Instead of wasting time making a well-built brass cylinder, he used the cylinder from a big brass syringe normally used to inject wax into dead bodies to prepare them for dissection by university medical students.

As Watt worked, a tiny pump unlike any ever built took shape. It was upside down with the piston near the foot of the cylinder and the piston rod ending in a hook.

The principle of the vacuum was proved by the experiment shown on these pages. The iron hemispheres (opposite) were locked together. Once the air was pumped out, two teams of horses could not pull the hemispheres apart.

The Industrial Revolution changed the face of the English countryside from the farming lands shown above to heavily populated areas near coalfields with factories and housing for workers.

Right: The movement of population from farming areas to cities continues today.

It Moves

At last, the connections were all made, and a test weight dangled on the end of the piston rod. Steam hissed through a pipe connected with a temporary boiler into a cylinder. This was tightly closed with a double skin that filled with steam. When wisps of steam appeared from the top, Watt knew everything was ready.

Carefully, he turned off the connection and pumped air out of the condenser, cooling it with water. Inside, he believed, a vacuum should form, sucking steam out of the upper part of the cylinder and creating a vacuum there too. And then, it happened. The test weight on the end of the rod began to move upward, pulled closer and closer to the cylinder by the piston rod.

Meanwhile, the rod itself vanished into the cylinder's interior, pushed in by the steam that had collected below the piston. That steam, like air, exerted a pressure against the piston's surface and drove it upward into the vacuum that had been created above. Best of all, the cylinder itself remained boiling hot, heated by the "steam jacket" that formed its double skin.

"A Perfect Steam Engine"

John Robison had been away from Glasgow during the weekend of his friend's great invention. He returned full of fresh ideas about the riddle that he'd left Watt pondering. Hurrying to Watt's home, he found his friend in a strange mood. Watt was sitting by the fire with a small tin box on his knees. Beside him, a soldering iron was heating on the flames. Robison chattered on but Watt—usually so warm, so enthusiastic—made little response. Staring into the fire, he seemed far away.

At last, putting the box on the floor, he cut Robison's chatter short. He looked down at the little

> "The fortunate thought occurred to him [Watt] of condensing the steam by cold in a separate vessel or apparatus, between which and the cylinder a communication was to be opened for that purpose every time the steam was to be condensed; while the cylinder itself might be preserved perpetually hot . . . . This capital improvement flashed on his mind at once, and filled him with rapture."
>
> Professor Black, recalling the invention of the separate condenser

box on the floor, then pushed it away with his foot, out of sight under a table. Robison fell silent, unable to decipher his friend's strange mood. Then he realized that Watt was simply exhausted from work.

Watt later told him everything—but not before Robison had learned from someone else the details of what his friend had created. "I had no doubt," he recalled, "that Mr. Watt had really made a perfect steam engine."

Watt's Friends

James Watt was twenty-nine when he had his great inspiration. Yet, he did not see it put to commercial use until he was forty. Between those two triumphs came eleven years of struggle, worry, disillusionment, and grief. On his own, he would probably have been overwhelmed by the difficulties he met, and his steam engine would have remained just a model. But the engineer of genius also had a gift for friendship, and it was Watt's friends who, in the end, saw him through.

They knew Watt was shy, sometimes thoughtless, sometimes maddeningly timid and hesitant. They also knew that he was modest, good-natured, and warm-hearted. These were the qualities that had first attracted men such as Robert Dick and Joseph Black to the craftsmen-mechanic in the university workshop. And it was the high opinion that Black and the rest held of Watt that inspired them to bring Watt's invention to the wider world of industry and commerce.

Need to Make a Living

After those momentous days in May 1765, Watt was obsessed with his new invention. As he once told someone, "I can think of nothing else but this engine." All the same, the little trial engines he put together on his workbench or by his fireside were simply models. They were not even full-scale working models, let alone something from which he could make a living. And the business of making a living was still his main concern. It had to be, since he had a family and, during that time, his usual money worries had become worse.

Watt's partner, who'd put money into the shop, had died. His death meant that Watt had to pay back all the money he'd been lent to his partner's heirs. This could mean selling his business to square his debt. As had happened before, Professor Black stepped in to help. Watt was not only his friend. The inventor was now, as everyone knew, working on something really important. The work had to go on. So, at first, Black lent Watt money to live on.

Black knew this was only a short-term solution—for one thing, he wasn't rich himself. He did, however, know a business owner and a mine-operator who was. This man, Black was convinced, would surely need a new, truly efficient pump!

This eighteenth century cartoon makes fun of steam power. Little did people know that "riding the steam" on a steam-powered railroad train would soon become a reality.

John Roebuck Lends a Hand

Without delay, the professor introduced Watt and his invention to John Roebuck. Roebuck was a scientist, industrialist, and landholder of the rich coal deposits that lay near Edinburgh, Scotland. Black imagined that Watt could put his pump at Roebuck's disposal. In return, Roebuck would give him the backing, workshop, and encouragement he needed to bring it from its trial stage to full working use.

Watt succeeded in building a full-scale version of his pumping engine and setting it up at a mine. But that was about as far as things went for the next nine years.

Part of the fault was Watt's. He hated having to be a boss and run a team of workers. He also didn't like the business of keeping on good terms with his new patron. Roebuck, however, was at fault, too. He knew all about Watt's need for a steady income. But, for some time, he personally did nothing to help ease his partner's financial problems. Instead, he actually encouraged Watt in a plan to leave instrument making and set up as surveyor.

Gathering Dust

Perhaps Roebuck hoped to get Watt's engine "on the cheap," by making sure that Watt was doing a job that paid well—surveying. If so, Roebuck was mistaken. Watt's career change took him all over the country, while his invention gathered dust in his workshop.

Roebuck did, however, do Watt two favors that were valuable. First, he helped Watt take out a patent on his machine. This meant, for the years of the patent's life, no one could copy the method Watt had invented for "lessening the consumption of steam and fuel in fire engines."

The patent itself, which was granted in 1769, formed part of the financial deal that Roebuck and Watt eventually made. Roebuck would pay off

Watt's debt to Black and, in return, would take two-thirds of any money the invention made.

Roebuck's second service was even more important. He introduced Watt to the man who could ensure that Watt's invention would reach the public—Matthew Boulton of Birmingham, England.

Boulton's "Manufactory"

Boulton, like Roebuck, was a wealthy industrialist. The business he had inherited from his father made ornamental metal goods. By the 1760s, the fashion world had made pierced steelwork the latest fad. Boulton supplied a wide variety of fashionable and expensive items—ornamental buttons, watch-chains, combs, sword hilts, and snuff boxes.

Production on this wide variety of items was very unusual at that time. Most craftwork—like the work Watt himself did—was slow, small scale, and workshop based. Boulton had decided to house all his craft workers under one roof, in a "manufactory" equipped with the latest, most efficient equipment money could buy.

The idea of a large-scale, centralized workplace was, at that time, very rare. Boulton, however, had done more than centralize, he had built the biggest factory in the Western world.

Chance of a Lifetime

Watt and Boulton met for the first time in 1768 and got along well from the start. Boulton, a jovial, confident, successful, and shrewd man took an instant liking to the engineer and surveyor who shared none of those traits. Watt, for his part, relaxed in the warmth of Boulton's friendliness, and responded with delight to his interest in the steam engine. Boulton, the man who'd had the vision to spend a fortune on his new-style premises, was very interested in this steam-powered invention.

With a sharp eye for good business deals, he realized that Watt's pump was the answer to the mine-owners prayers. And they weren't the only businesspeople who needed an efficient pump.

Manufacturing the Scotsman's machine would be a highly profitable business, Boulton was sure of it. All he had to do was propose a partnership to the young engineer.

Watt would have jumped at the chance—except for the fact that he was tied to Roebuck by his debts and agreements. The three men tried to negotiate a deal that pleased everyone, but the negotiations fell through. In 1771, Watt abandoned the pump project and spent the next few years as a full-time surveyor, constructing canals across Scotland.

Canal building, like that shown here, was the main work of civil engineers in the eighteenth century. During Watt's six years as a canal surveyor, he invented a micrometer for judging distances and heights—knowledge that was critical to building these "water highways."

The Final Blow?

Roebuck begged Watt to leave surveying and come back to his workshop. But Watt had to provide for himself, his wife, and their three children. He had to earn a practical, day-to-day living. The love affair with the steam engine was over. He was now a surveyor.

Then, in March 1773, Roebuck went bankrupt. To thirty-seven-year old Watt, it must have seemed like the end to his life's great dream. But it was the opposite. The way was now open for Boulton to buy Roebuck's two-thirds share in Watt's patent, which he did in August 1773.

The next month, something happened that finally shook Watt free from surveying, from Scotland, and from his roots forever. His wife Margaret was pregnant. As gales swept the Scottish Highlands, word reached Watt that his wife was desperately ill. He set out at once on a nightmarish journey back to Glasgow, riding through the storm. But, fast as he could travel, he arrived too late. Margaret and the baby were dead.

In many ways, Margaret had played as large a part as his friends had in keeping Watt's spirits up during the difficult years. She constantly urged him to keep his faith in himself. "I beg you would not make yourself uneasy, though things should not succeed to your wish," she had once written to him. "If it [the steam engine] will not do, something else will. Never despair."

The next spring, when his grief eased, Watt packed up his belongings and headed south to Birmingham, where his future lay.

Going Public

In early March 1776, the directors of the Bentley Mining Company talked among themselves as they prepared to view their newest equipment. Would it

Before railroads were built in the nineteenth century, canals like the one shown below were the main means of transporting passengers and good in many areas of the world, including the young United States.

work? Would it prove that their decision to scrap their half-built Newcomen pump for this latest model was right? How would the demonstration affect Mr. Bentley, the owner? How would it affect the inventor, his partner, and all the distinguished visitors who were gathering to see the machine in all its full-scale glory?

They'd have been more nervous still if they'd known the press was present, too. A correspondent from the local paper was already composing lines in his head as, eyes alert and ears open, he moved among the assembled crowd. The Boulton & Watt pumping engine—capable, so it was said, of emptying a mine three hundred feet deep—was about to make its first-ever public performance.

From every side, details rained down on the correspondent. Watt pumping engines, he was told, were different from anything that had come before. They used only a quarter of the fuel of a Newcomen engine to do a similar job. The engine had taken its inventor years of work to develop. "Many years of study," the newspaper later reported, "and a great variety of expensive and laborious experiments."

The cylinder, the correspondent learned, was fifty inches across, and had been made by the best ironmaster in Britain, John Wilkinson. Not long before, Wilkinson had invented a way of making cannon barrels that were perfectly round inside — all along their length. He'd now brought the same skill to making the main component of the Boulton & Watt engine. In fact, he'd even installed a Watt machine at his own workshop to act as a gigantic bellows.

All the precision work—the valves, pistons, connections, and the condenser itself—had come from the Birmingham Soho Manufactory where Watt and Boulton were now partners. The machine set before the crowd was the second to emerge from the special section that Boulton had set up at Soho to house the new business. Four more steam engines, the newspaper correspondent learned, were nearly ready, and more were planned.

The Beam Swings Down

Around the new engine house, an excited crowd formed. Inside, an engineer bounced around before the towering equipment, pulling levers, opening and closing valves. Above him, like the jutting arm of a gallows, loomed the great beam that would soon seesaw on its pivot, acting as the handle to work the new pump.

The Bentley engine in this photo was installed in a Birmingham factory in 1777.

This painting shows Matthew Boulton's Soho "manufactory" in Birmingham, England. Boulton and Watt set up special departments in the factory to make parts for their engines.

Deftly, the engineer closed a sequence of valves, checked a gauge, pulled a lever, then paused. Finally, he stretched out his arm and opened a new valve. And, high overhead, the giant pump-handle suddenly swung downward.

Down it came—"the length of the Stroke is 7 feet" noted the newspaper correspondent—and up it went again. And down it plunged, and up, and down, all with great thudding strokes. The chains clanked, the wooden timbers creaked and groaned, the walls of the engine house shook. Deafened and entranced, the crowd watched the beam's rise and fall. Few could have known that they were witnessing the birth of the Industrial Revolution. Meanwhile, down in the waterlogged pit, the water level began to drop.

The Age of Steam

In less than an hour, the show was over. The pit, which had once stood fifty-seven feet deep in water, was now empty. As the great beam made its last descent, the engineer closed off valves and shut the incredible machine down. The crowd, chattering excitedly, made its way off to the celebration dinner.

Behind them, the Bentley Company's new purchase stood silent again, awaiting the moment when it would be put to work in earnest. The new engine was a success from the start. Sometimes things went wrong—valves broke, steam leaked from casings, or the engineers opened the wrong valve. All the same, orders for Boulton & Watt engines came in from all over the country. And requests were already coming in from other countries.

Cornish mine owners wanted a fuel-saving Watt engine more than anyone else because they mined copper and tin, not coal. Instead of running their pumps on the very material they dug up, they had to bring in every lump of fuel from outside. The cost was huge, and there was nothing they could do about it—until the Watt engine came on the scene.

At first, they tried to steal the design. Not long after the Bentley engine started work, a group of Cornishmen came to see it. When they left, one of them took with him a drawing that showed how everything worked. Watt soon discovered the theft. Boulton, furious, wasted no time in accusing his visitors with a crime. Shamefacedly, they told him the drawing had been picked up by mistake. The man who'd taken it was a mine manager called Richard Trevithick. This was a name that Watt was to hear again.

This portrait of James Watt was painted in 1792, when Watt was fifty-six years old and the wealthy part-owner of a prosperous business.

Enough for a Lifetime

In the end, the Cornish had to settle for buying the machine, so they started by ordering two. Watt took charge of the installation. Unfortunately, he soon found that this project caused him great hardship and discomfort.

Opposite: *This sketch gives a partial view of Heathfield Hall, Watt's home near Birmingham where he lived throughout the later part of his life.*

Just getting there was horrendous. The inventor, who'd recently married again, set off with his new wife Ann in the summer of 1777. The two hundred-mile journey took them four days. The Watts did not find the Cornish people to be hospitable. Instead, most were rude, boorish, and ignorant. "The enginemen actually eat the grease for the engine!" Watt wrote despairingly to his Birmingham friends. Worse, many were suspicious of this outsider and his contraption.

Watt strived to ease the Cornish miners' doubts and as he brought the two new engines to working order. He found the second task much easier. He hated the business of making contacts, chatting, and generally selling himself and his machine. But it was all part of being in business. And, in Cornwall, it was weary work.

Trevithick was disrespectful. The other managers were hostile, stupid, or both. Thus it was an anxious moment when one machine was ready to run a month after Watt's arrival. It performed well, and went on functioning. The other went into operation a few months later.

Wanted: New Markets

James Watt had shown the world how to harness steam power efficiently. As far as he was concerned, that was enough. He had his hands full, running the Cornish end of the business and making sure that his pump met the demands made on it. But Boulton, ambitious as ever, thought differently. He knew that Cornwall was only one market among many. Sooner or later, most of the Cornish mines would have Watt pumps. What would happen to sales then?

The partnership had to expand, open up new markets, and continue to develop machines that were more powerful and efficient. Boulton also knew

"The earth, which had been burrowed out by those human rabbits in their search after tin, lay around in huge ungainly heaps . . . dirt and slush, and pools of water confined by muddy dams, abounded on every side; muddy men, with muddy carts and muddy horses, slowly crawled hither and thither."

Conditions above ground at Cornish tin mines, around the time that Watt knew them

42

where these machines might be used. By this time, other "manufactories" were springing up. Some made heavy ironware. Others produced pottery. Still others produced textiles, especially cotton textiles.

Cotton, Mills, and Rotary Motion

The cotton industry was then very new. Like mining, it was flourishing, and for a similar reason. New machines such as Richard Arkwright's mechanized spinning frame were improving the productivity of textile manufacture beyond imagination. True, the spinning machines in Arkwright's chain of textile mills were powered by water. But everyone knew that couldn't last forever

This was already in Boulton's mind as he watched the Bentley pump go into action. By that time, the local newspaperman reported, he was planning to provide engines to meet "almost all purposes where mechanical power is required, whether great or small, or where the motion wanted is either rotatory or reciprocating."

"Rotatory" was obviously the next step. Watt's pump, like Newcomen's before it, was a reciprocating engine. Its movement was two-way only: in and out, up and down, side to side. But many machines—starting with the flourmill—operated on the rotary principal. They went round and round. Could a Watt engine be built that worked like that?

"Steam Mill Mad"

In June 1781, Boulton wrote a tactful letter to his partner that has since become famous. "The people in London, Manchester and Birmingham," he told Watt, "are steam mill mad. I don't mean to hurry you but I think in the course of a month or two, we should determine to take out a patent for certain methods of producing rotative motion . . . .

A massive iron-making plant is shown here. Along with steam, iron was one of the foundations of the Industrial Revolution. Without iron, steam engines and later railways would not have been possible.

Boulton's gentle but firm approach to his partner produced immediate results. Watt, aged forty-five, rose to the new challenge, working long hours in his workshop at the manufactory. By October, he'd come up with a brand-new device that converted power into a rotary movement. It had to be a new device, because someone else had already taken out a patent on the most obvious way of doing the job, by using a crank.

A crank is a wheel attached to a hinged rod. A to-and-fro movement of the rod will make the wheel go round, and vice versa. Barred from using this simple idea, Watt worked out something equally simple. He attached the "pump-handle," the overhead beam, to a long rod that ended in a small-notched wheel. The beam's up-and-down movement made this wheel move round another one, which in its turn rotated a much larger wheel.

Thanks to this "sun-and-planet" gear, in which one wheel rotated round another, the original Boulton & Watt steam engine could be quickly transformed into the much more versatile rotative model. But Watt did not stop there. The new-style steam engine that he patented in 1782 not only worked by rotary motion, it worked twice as efficiently.

Pull-push Action

Both Newcomen's pump and Watt's first engine had been "single acting." The power that drove them only functioned in one direction. It pulled the "pump-handle" down, at its end nearest the cylinder. It did not, however, push it up. Gravity did that, acting on the other end of the beam when the pull on the engine end was abandoned.

By rearranging its valve system, Watt had produced an engine that exerted power in two directions. This "double-acting" engine pulled the beam down and pushed it up again.

This pull-push action made another change necessary. Until that point, the piston rod and the beam had been joined by a flexible chain. This would not work now since the chain could not transmit the upward thrust of the "push" movement. Watt now faced the problem of linking something that moved up and down—the piston rod—with something that moved through an arc of a circle.

Straight Line and Curve

The problem might sound trivial, but it was very difficult. Confined to its up-and-down path, the rod cannot move sideways at all. The beam-end, however, travels in a sideways curve. Somehow, Watt had to bring the rod's straight line and the beam's curve together. And he had to keep them together through all the different positions the engine's power created.

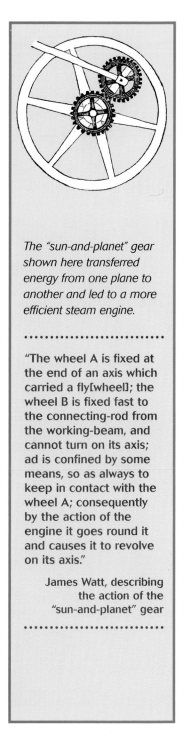

The "sun-and-planet" gear shown here transferred energy from one plane to another and led to a more efficient steam engine.

• •

"The wheel A is fixed at the end of an axis which carried a fly[wheel]; the wheel B is fixed fast to the connecting-rod from the working-beam, and cannot turn on its axis; ad is confined by some means, so as always to keep in contact with the wheel A; consequently by the action of the engine it goes round it and causes it to revolve on its axis."

James Watt, describing the action of the "sun-and-planet" gear

• •

Watt first tried inter-connecting notches, like the ones on the gears. But the teeth of the notch system kept breaking. Something else was needed, and Watt started playing with the geometry of the problem. The beam-end traced an arc of one circle. Suppose a similar arc was traced of another circle, back-to-back under the first one. The two arcs would not, of course, make a straight line. But they were not far off.

The second circle would be traced by the end of another beam, or rod or anything straight. Then the moving ends of the two rods could be linked by a third. If the first rod—the beam—were moved through its usual arc, the second one would move as well. The short third rod, at its ends, copied the arcs of the other two. There was a point along its length, however, at which it moved in almost a straight line, unlike anything else in the whole arrangement.

"A Probable Thing to Succeed"

Watt wrote to Boulton on June 30, giving tentative news of success. "I have started a new hare!" he joked. "I have got a glimpse of a method of causing a piston-rod to move up and down perpendicularly, by only fixing it to a piece of iron upon the beam . . . . I have only tried it in a slight model yet, so cannot build upon it, though I think it a very probable thing to succeed."

Succeed it did. That single point on the third connecting rod was the place where the straight line and the circle met. When attached to it, the piston transmitted all its up-and-down thrust to the end of the beam. And the beam, moving along its arc, swung into the air. In its final form, the equipment was more complicated but much more compact. Years later, when Watt recalled the movement of its polished parallel rods, he still glowed with pride.

"I am more proud of the parallel motion than of any other mechanical invention I have ever made," he told his son, also named James.

Towering Achievements

The sun-and-planet gears, the double-acting engine, the parallel motion device—any one of these would have brought the highest distinction to an inventor. Taken together, with the initial invention of the separate condenser, they add up to a towering achievement. Still, they are only part of what James Watt created after he joined Boulton.

Boulton went far beyond giving his partner financial security. He also gave him friendship, encouragement, and an endlessly patient ear. Under his genial influence, the inventor's creativity flourished as never before.

There was, for instance, his patent copying process, which he developed at the end of the 1770s. This was years before the typewriter took a lot of the drudgery out of business correspondence, and long before the photocopier removed much of the rest.

The only way that Boulton and Watt could make copies of the letters they wrote was to copy them out themselves—by hand. It was a time-wasting, tedious chore. Watt decided that they needed a good letter-copying method. Very quickly he produced a whole letter-copying system, complete with special inks, special paper, and special presses. After writing a letter, the writer would carefully press a sheet of thin, absorbent paper down on top of the still-wet ink. When this upper sheet was peeled off, it carried a "transfer" of the letter, written in back-to-front, mirror-image script. All the reader then had to do was turn the paper over. Because the paper was so thin, the writing showed through from the back the right way.

"I have fallen on a way of copying writing chemically.... I can copy a whole-sheet letter in five minutes."

James Watt, on his copying process

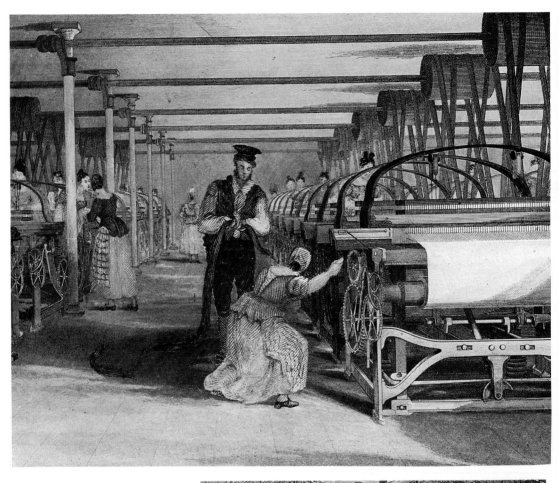

Above: *Steam power in textile mills led to the production of cheap cloth—and to poor working conditions for women and children as shown in this drawing.*

Right: *James Nasmyth's steam hammer, invented 1839, made it possible to forge large machine parts with a degree of accuracy once thought impossible.*

Watt wasn't the only busy person to rebel against the need for hand copying. So Boulton manufactured and promoted his partner's latest inspiration, and sold over a hundred in the first year alone. The Watt copier soon became part of standard business practice.

How Powerful Is a Horse?

Another spin-off from Watt's main work has been in use much longer. In 1782, a customer ordered an engine to drive a sawmill. He explained what he wanted in terms of the amount of work that could be done by a horse walking around a treadmill. The engine was to have the power of about twelve horses.

While this figure meant something to the mill-owner, it was hardly exact enough for Watt. Here was something that had to be worked out properly. How much power did a horse really exert?

Watt studied the sawmill's figures: the distance a horse walked in a minute, the weight lifted by the machine it drove, and so on. He started calculating, and finally worked out that a horse could lift 33,000 pounds the distance of one foot in one minute. The inventor could now estimate how powerful the engine needed to be. Also, he could now describe how powerful any of his machines were and price them accordingly. He had defined "horsepower," a standard unit by which power is still measured. The international measurement system, however, uses a different unit for measuring power. It is called the watt.

Revolution in Industry

Watt continued to improve on his own inventions through middle age. Meanwhile, the fame of his greatest invention—the steam engine—was increasing by the year. Boulton's great gamble was paying off brilliantly, machines and the factories

"It has armed the feeble hand . . . with a power to which no limits can be assigned; completed the dominion of mind over the most refractory qualities of matter; and laid a sure foundation for all those future miracles of mechanic power which to aid and reward the labors of after generations."

James Watt's steam engine, described in his obituary, 1819

"The great, unwearying power of the Watt engine made possible the mechanization of production methods upon a scale that was inconceivable before."

L.T.C. Rolt, from his biography, "James Watt"

This illustration from a brochure printed in 1851 for the Great Exhibition in London, shows the range of machinery that British industry had created. Steam made Great Britain the world's leading industrial power until about 1880 when the United States took the lead.

that housed them were revolutionizing industries. Among the industries that received the greatest boost from steam power was textiles.

Among textile factory owners demand was now growing for something more powerful and much less chancy than a water wheel to turn spindles and bobbins. The Boulton & Watt rotative engine was everything they wanted—and more. A factory equipped with a power source like that could be built wherever the owner wished. Producers, if they paid Boulton & Watt's terms, could free themselves forever from their old reliance on water, weather, and muscle power.

For the first time in history, workers could control their environment.

Left: *The steam engine played an important part in the development of the iron industry. Thanks to steam, the British iron industry produced four times more iron in 1804 than it did in 1788, before steam engines were widely used.*

By 1800, when Watt's main patent finally ran out, eighty-four British cotton mills were using Boulton & Watt engines. So were some wool mills, suddenly aware of the threat posed by their new rivals. And the flour-milling industry had begun to copy their example.

Whether they liked it or hated it—and many industries hated the initial expense—the steam engine and the huge amounts of power it made available were the keys to any industry's future.

Planning to Enjoy Himself

The expiration of the patent also marked the formal end of the Boulton & Watt partnership. The two friends were now getting old—Boulton was seventy-two, Watt sixty-four. Their sons had taken over Soho's engine-making operations. Even so, Boulton did not think of retiring. He plunged into a scheme for building machinery to mint coins. But Watt had different plans.

Everything that once seemed far out of reach had now been granted to him—wealth, fame, and the recognition of his profession and his country. He even had good health. Happiness and good fortune, coming late but coming in the end, had banished the migraines that once made life a misery. He was fit to enjoy retirement, and he did just that.

Happy in a new house he'd built for himself, he spent the last nineteen years of his life doing all the things he liked best. He read and researched. He planned a garden and planted it. He spent hours in the workshop he'd rigged up for himself in the attic.

Here, surrounded by the tools he treasured all his life, he worked on his latest scheme—a machine for copying pieces of sculpture. This newest "hare" claimed all his attention, just as the others had. It absorbed him so much that often he didn't even come downstairs for meals. It would

TREVITHICKS,
PORTABLE STEAM ENGINE.

Catch me who can.

Mechanical Power Subduing
Animal Speed.

have meant tidying himself up, and he couldn't really be bothered.

Even before the century ended, his friends had begun dying. Black was the first to go, then Robison, and then, in 1809, Boulton himself. Richard Trevithick, Watt's old adversary in Cornwall, died too. But Trevithick's role as an irritant to the firm of Boulton & Watt soon passed to his son, also named Richard and—like Watt himself—an engineer.

Before the Watt patent expired, the younger Richard Trevithick began building steam engines with Watt-style separate condensers that harnessed a property of steam that Watt had not—its expansive power. Soon, he was designing rotative steam engines that also worked on this high-pressure principle.

One of these was a full-sized, self-propelled steam-carriage. In 1804, this engine trundled along nine and a half miles of railed tracks in South Wales, pulling a train loaded with seventy passengers and ten tons of iron. It was the world's first railway locomotive.

Here was a rival who could put the Soho operation out of business for good! But the dangers of high-pressure steam discouraged possible buyers. One steam engine exploded, killing four men, and Trevithick later left England to seek his fortune in Peru. Meanwhile, Watt had his mind on his greenhouses, and his tree planting, and the tools in his attic. Watt died at age eighty-three, on August 25, 1819, and was buried close to his old partner, Matthew Boulton.

Legacy to the World

By increasing the power of humans, James Watt led the modern world to some of its greatest changes. First came the Industrial Revolution—the shift from home-based crafts to factory-based production. His

Opposite: *This portrait shows Richard Trevithick, the son of Watt's old Cornish antagonist. A poster from 1808 advertises Trevithick's famous steam engine.*

• •

"The darkest side of this rapid power revolution was that it robbed the craftsman's hands of their cunning and subjected him to the swift, inhuman rhythm of the new machines."

L.T.C Rolt, from his biography, "James Watt"

• •

Steam changed the face of transportation in the 1800s. The painting above shows Delta Queen carrying passengers and goods down the Mississippi River. Steam railways changed the face of the English countryside as well, with trains traveling along newly built bridges, tunnels and viaducts like the one shown at right in Manchester, England.

work also led to a revolution in travel and communications, as well as huge population shifts when new factories were set up and people moved to work in them.

The engines Watt built and the power he harnessed set these changes in motion long before he died. Later, as the process of change spread, his legacy transformed people's lives more than he could have imagined. His overall vision, coupled with his unerring eye, shaped the nineteenth century as surely as if he'd lived through it.

Many changes brought about by Watt came very fast. One of the biggest changes was simply that the pace of change itself increased. For the bewildered onlookers of the early nineteenth century, even the earliest changes seemed to gather momentum as years passed.

For instance, Trevithick's seventy passengers took their historic journey in 1804. Only four years later, his "Catch me who can" locomotive, which advertised itself as "Mechanical Power

In the United States, steam-driven locomotives had "cowcatchers" in front of the wheels. These kept cattle that wandered onto the track from falling beneath the wheels and stopping the train. The funnels on the smokestacks were designed to keep sparks from escaping and causing fires.

Subduing Animal Speed," was carrying Londoners on joyrides around a circular track.

In 1814, an engineer, George Stephenson, produced a steam locomotive that hauled an eight-wagon train of coal uphill. In 1825, his more famous *Locomotion* carried a group of passengers along the world's first-ever public rail line. Five years later, the more celebrated *Rocket* made its prize-winning run on the Manchester and Liverpool Railway built by Stephenson himself giving the world its first regular passenger rail service.

The Manchester and Liverpool railway was soon joined by others. By 1850—only half a century from that first ponderous trip achieved by Trevithick's engine—rail lines ran across Britain.

Race of the Steamships

Change came equally fast with water transport—and, as with Watt's own steam engine, the story started in Scotland. Steam was first used to power a ship in 1801, when the idea of the steam-powered paddle wheel was applied to a canal boat. The example set by this first paddle steamer was quickly copied, especially in the United States, and, in 1819, the paddle-steamer *Savannah* made history by becoming the first steamship to cross the Atlantic Ocean.

Two centuries earlier, this journey had taken two months or more. By 1838, when the paddle steamers *Sirius* and *Great Western* challenged each other to an epic race, the time had been cut to well under three weeks. A hundred years later, it had dropped to three days.

Thanks to steam power, distance and time had broken their old links with wind, terrain, and horses' hooves. To nineteenth century onlookers, it must have seemed that the world was shrinking before their eyes.

The Making of Industry

These major changes included an extraordinary improvement in communications, a massive increase in trade, an explosion in numbers emigrating to the New World, and some enormous changes in the attitudes of the people left in the Old World. No longer was London—or Paris, or Berlin—like something out of a fable, a place from which few fortune-seekers returned. Country dwellers could now work there, settle there, marry there, and still return to see their families back home.

Immense though those changes were, they were dwarfed by those that arose from steam power's impact on industry. In fact, steam power didn't so much change industry as create it.

In Germany, the change took place in the 1850s and 1860s when there was a period of rapid growth. The railways expanded and basic industries, such as mining, metals, textiles, and iron, became large-scale concerns.

"Workshop of the World"

The power revolution did not confine itself to mining, iron making, and textile manufacture. Steel, smelted from iron, was beaten, then rolled or shaped on steam-powered machines. In the fields, steam-threshing machines quickly completed a task that, by hand, could take from harvest time until Christmas. Newspapers were printed on steam-driven presses. After the mid-century invention of the sewing machine, parts of the clothing industry changed over to sewing clothes by steam.

Great Britain, home of the technology that made industry possible, earned the nickname "Workshop of the World." By the end of the nineteenth century, industrial world leadership had passed to Germany, then to the United States. By this time, however,

Britain had changed roles to become the world's most powerful political force.

Other Western nations acquired empires of their own, and this land grabbing was also linked to the revolution steam had brought about. All these nations needed raw materials to feed their industries' machines. They also needed places where they could sell their industrial products. An empire met both these needs.

Opposite and above:
Steam paved the way for the development of electric power. Electricity is generated in large plants like these by using coal, oil, natural gas, or nuclear fuel to raise steam pressure that drives a turbine that in turn drives a generator.

Cities

Steam power also changed the map of every country in which it took root. In 1750, for instance, Birmingham, the town where Matthew Boulton was working in his family firm, had a population of about 30,000 people. By 1801, the year after his partnership with Watt ended, the town's population had doubled. By the mid-century, it had shot up to well over 200,000. The same was true throughout the industrialized world. In Germany, the population of Berlin increased by 100,000 between 1840 and 1850.

Slowly, Europeans and their descendants elsewhere were giving up centuries-old links with the land. Instead, they were building societies based on a different way of life. Now they were collected together in a town.

Past and Future

The rise of communities created issues and opportunities vastly different from those of rural life. Housing, health care, and education were issues more easily addressed when they affected people living closely together.

Economically, community living meant more efficient ways of doing business. Large numbers of customers in a small area meant fewer transportation and production costs for businesses.

In 1882, a business entrepreneur and inventor, Thomas A. Edison found it worth his while to sell New York a system for bringing electrical power into the home. Edison bridged the technology gap between Watt's time and our own. Electricity brought the world out of the Age of Steam, and prepared the way for the high technology of the late 1900's. Edison's system itself, however, depended on steam for generating electricity. The same is true of some power stations today.

James Watt, the engineer who shaped our past, will surely continue to shape our future far into the twenty-first century.

Timeline

1698	Thomas Savery patents his "Miner's Friend:" a water pump powered by creating and then condensing steam so as to form a vacuum.
1712	Thomas Newcomen sets up his first "atmospheric engine"—a fully-functioning steam pump.
1736	**Jan 19:** James Watt is born in Greenock, Scotland.
1755	Watt leaves Scotland to seek training as an instrument-maker in London. He is taken on by John Morgan of Cornhill.
1756	His training completed, Watt returns to Scotland and repairs an instrument collection for Glasgow University.
1757	Glasgow University sets Watt up as its official "Mathematical Instrument Maker," with a shop in the university grounds.
1763–4	Professor John Anderson brings Watt a model of a Newcomen pump for repair. Watt realizes that the pump works inefficiently because its cylinder has to be cooled and re-heated with every stroke.
1765	**May:** Watt, aged twenty-nine, works out the solution to the pump problem: a separate cooling chamber, or condenser. Later that year, he is introduced to scientist and industrialist John Roebuck, who is interest in developing Watt's invention for commercial use.
1769	Watt patents his "New Method of Lessening the Consumption of Steam and Fuel in Fire Engines." In the same year, Richard Arkwright patents his water-powered spinning machine, the "Water Frame."
1774	Watt, aged thirty-eight, moves from Scotland to Birmingham, England, and starts work at the Soho Manufactory as the partner of Matthew Boulton, bringing the steam engine he has designed into production.
1776	The Boulton & Watt steam pump makes its first working appearance in public, at the Bloomsfield Colliery.
1777	Watt travels to Cornwall to set up Boulton & Watt pumps at two mines.
1781	Watt patents his double-acting engine. In the same year, he devises a standard unit of measurement for power: the horsepower.
1784	Watt's parallel motion device is patented.

1785	Edmund Cartwright, a clergyman, patents his powered weaving-loom. Together with powered spinning machines, already introduced, improved versions of the power-loom will play a leading role in taking manufacturing industries out of the home and into factories.
1800	Watt's patent on his steam engine runs out. The Boulton & Watt partnership comes to an end, and sixty-four-year-old Watt retires.
1804	The world's first steam-powered railway locomotive, designed by Richard Trevithick, hauls a load of ten tons of iron and around seventy people over a distance of more than nine miles.
1819	**Aug 25:** James Watt dies, aged eighty-three.

Glossary

Arc A section of a circle's circumference.

"Atmospheric Engine" A machine powered by the pressure of the earth's atmosphere (the air), acting on a vacuum produced by condensing steam: the name given to Newcomen's pumping engine. Although Watt's engine used steam rather than air, it worked in the same basic way. *See condenser.*

Boiler The part of a steam engine where water is converted into steam. The water in the boiler is heated until it boils.

Condense, condenser When steam is cooled, it condenses, or turns back to water. Watt's greatest achievement was the invention of a separate cooling-chamber, or condenser, for the Newcomen pump.

Double-acting engine See single-acting engine.

Energy The capacity to do work.

Horsepower Unit of measurement for power used in the British (imperial) measurement system. One horsepower equals 745.7 watts (see Watt).

Industrial Revolution The massive changeover from home-based systems of production to factory-based ones that was pioneered in Britain in the late eighteenth and early nineteenth centuries. The key to change was the introduction of powered machines (using water or steam power) to do work previously done by hand, such as spinning and weaving.

"Manufactory" A place where goods are made; the original version of the word "factory."

Patent Legal protection, lasting for a fixed length of time, for an invention. While the patent lasts, only the patent-holder has the right to make goods using the invention, and to market them.

Piston, piston-rod A piston is a circular piece of metal, cut to fit closely inside a cylinder and free to move up and down. The piston rod is a rod attached at right angles to the piston.

Pivot A short rod on which something turns.

Power In scientific language, the rate at which work is done, or energy is used up or produced. In ordinary speech, "power" is often given the meaning that actually belongs to "energy:" the ability to do work. A machine that is "powered" by steam in fact a machine that uses the energy of steam to do the job it was designed for.

Pressure Force exerted against something. The piston of the Newcomen pump was driven down into the pump's cylinder by the pressure of the atmosphere exerted against its upper surface.

Quadrant An instrument for measuring angles.

Reciprocating Two-way, straight-line motion: up and down, or side to side. Compare with rotary.

Rotary, rotative Circular motion; an engine operating in this way.

Single-acting/double-acting engines In a single-acting engine, pressure is exerted on the piston on one side only: the upper one, in the case of the Newcomen, and early Watt pumps. In double-acting engines, like the later Boulton & Watt ones, the pressure is exerted, first on one side of the piston, then on the other.

Steam The gas into which water turns when it is boiled. When this happens, its volume expands 1700 times. When steam in a container is condensed, it contracts again, creating a vacuum in the space it once filled. Both Newcomen and Watt based their engine designs on this vacuum-creating property of steam. Later on, however, engineers changed over to exploiting steam's expansive power. Early examples of this use of high-pressure steam include the first railway locomotives.

Sun-and-planet gear A gear system involving two wheels, one of which drives the other by moving around it.

Turbine A slatted wheel or circular device turned by the movement of a fluid or gas over the slats. A steam turbine is driven by steam.

Vacuum Space, which has been totally or to a large extent emptied of matter.

Valve A device which can be opened and closed (either by hand or automatically) to control the movement of fluid or gas through a narrow passage.

Watt The International System (SI) unit of power, named after James Watt. One watt is equal to one joule per second. (The joule is the SI unit of energy.)

For More Information

Books

Champion, Neil. *James Watt* (Groundbreakers). Westport, CT: Heinemann Library, 2000.

Pollard, Michael. *The Industrial Revolution* (Ideas that Changed the World). New York: Chelsea House, 1995.

Sproule, Anna. *Thomas A. Edison: The World's Greatest Inventor* (Giants of Science). Woodbridge, CT: Blackbirch Press, Inc., 2000.

Web Site

James Watt—Learn more about the life of James Watt. This site features links to other Web pages with information about the inventor: www.ideafinder.com/history/inventors/watt.htm

Index